Tía Loves You

By Mayra Medrano
Hernandez

Personally dedicated to my nieces and nephews. I love you all so much...

Because of you I am a tia. Being a sister is great, but being your tía is much more fun!

Cuándo te miro a ti y tú me miras a mi, I can already see all the wonderful things you'll be.

I hope you discover all that there is to see, and that you become anyone that you want to be. Te voy a amar for whoever you will be.

12

I may not always be by your side, but just know I am still with you, watching you from where I am.

Cheering you on I love watching you grow and be yourself. I can't wait to watch your story unfold.

Never forget I am just a call away, we'll be best buddies like nachos and cheese. Just give me a call and I will be there.

Elotes
Raspados
Fruta
Churros
PALERMO, CA

Juntos we will have delicioso treats and have lots of fun. Riendo y jugando until our day's done.

My wish for you is to grow up strong and healthy, and that all your dreams come true. May you always have courage and be kind. Remember más grande el corazón mas amor tendrá.

You may have many aunties, but just know shhhh...I love you the most! Mi corazón is full of love and I hope you know, mi amor goes with you wherever you go.

My happiness is being your aunt, never forget te quiero mucho. But for now sleep tight pumpkin pie, good night kisses, y que duermas con los angelitos.
Tía loves you.

www.ingramcontent.com/pod-product-compliance
Ingram Content Group UK Ltd.
Pitfield, Milton Keynes, MK11 3LW, UK
UKHW060115300726
14090UKWH00002B/212

* 9 7 9 8 2 1 8 4 7 7 2 9 5 *